Ward

by Iain Gray

Lang**Syne**

PUBLISHING

WRITING *to* REMEMBER

Lang**Syne**

PUBLISHING

WRITING *to* REMEMBER

Vineyard Business Centre,
Pathhead, Midlothian EH37 5XP
Tel: 01875 321 203 Fax: 01875 321 233
E-mail: info@lang-syne.co.uk
www.langsyneshop.co.uk

Design by Dorothy Meikle
Printed by Ricoh Print Scotland
© Lang Syne Publishers Ltd 2011

ISBN 978-1-85217-413-2

Ward

MOTTO:
Faithful even to death.

CREST:
A wolf's head.

NAME variations include:
Macanward
MacAward
Macward
McWard
Mac an Bháird *(Gaelic)*

Chapter one:
Origins of Irish surnames

**According to an old saying, there are two types of Irish –
those who actually are Irish and those who wish they were.**

This sentiment is only one example of the allure that the
high romance and drama of the proud nation's history holds
for thousands of people scattered across the world today.

It's a sad fact, however, that the vast majority of Irish
surnames are found far beyond Irish shores, rather than on
the Emerald Isle itself.

The population stood at around eight million souls in
1841, but today it stands at fewer than six million.

This is mainly a tragic consequence of the potato
famine, also known as the Great Hunger, which devastated
Ireland between 1845 and 1849.

The Irish peasantry had become almost wholly reliant
for basic sustenance on the potato, first introduced from the
Americas in the seventeenth century.

When the crop was hit by a blight, at least 800,000
people starved to death while an estimated two million
others were forced to seek a new life far from their native
shores – particularly in America, Canada, and Australia.

The effects of the potato blight continued until about
1851, by which time a firm pattern of emigration had
become established.

Ireland's loss, however, was to the gain of the countries in which the immigrants settled, contributing enormously, as their descendants do today, to the well being of the nations in which their forefathers settled.

But those who were forced through dire circumstance to establish a new life in foreign parts never forgot their roots, or the proud heritage and traditions of the land that gave them birth.

Nor do their descendants.

It is a heritage that is inextricably bound up in the colourful variety of Irish names themselves – and the origin and history of these names forms an integral part of the vibrant drama that is the nation's history, one of both glorious fortune and tragic misfortune.

This history is well documented, and one of the most important and fascinating of the earliest sources are *The Annals of the Four Masters*, compiled between 1632 and 1636 by four friars at the Franciscan Monastery in County Donegal.

Compiled from earlier sources, and purporting to go back to the Biblical Deluge, much of the material takes in the mythological origins and history of Ireland and the Irish.

This includes tales of successive waves of invaders and settlers such as the Fomorians, the Partholonians, the Nemedians, the Fir Bolgs, the Tuatha De Danann, and the Laigain.

Of particular interest are the *Milesian Genealogies*,

because the majority of Irish clans today claim a descent from either Heremon, Ir, or Heber – three of the sons of Milesius, a king of what is now modern day Spain.

These sons invaded Ireland in the second millennium B.C, apparently in fulfilment of a mysterious prophecy received by their father.

This Milesian lineage is said to have ruled Ireland for nearly 3,000 years, until the island came under the sway of England's King Henry II in 1171 following what is known as the Cambro-Norman invasion.

This is an important date not only in Irish history in general, but for the effect the invasion subsequently had for Irish surnames.

'Cambro' comes from the Welsh, and 'Cambro-Norman' describes those Welsh knights of Norman origin who invaded Ireland.

But they were invaders who stayed, inter-marrying with the native Irish population and founding their own proud dynasties that bore Cambro-Norman names such as Archer, Barbour, Brannagh, Fitzgerald, Fitzgibbon, Fleming, Joyce, Plunkett, and Walsh – to name only a few.

These 'Cambro-Norman' surnames that still flourish throughout the world today form one of the three main categories in which Irish names can be placed – those of Gaelic-Irish, Cambro-Norman, and Anglo-Irish.

Previous to the Cambro-Norman invasion of the twelfth century, and throughout the earlier invasions and settlement of those wild bands of sea rovers known as the Vikings in the eighth and ninth centuries, the population of the island was relatively small, and it was normal for a person to be identified through the use of only a forename.

But as population gradually increased and there were many more people with the same forename, surnames were adopted to distinguish one person, or one community, from another.

Individuals identified themselves with their own particular tribe, or 'tuath', and this tribe – that also became known as a clann, or clan – took its name from some distinguished ancestor who had founded the clan.

The Gaelic-Irish form of the name Kelly, for example, is Ó Ceallaigh, or O'Kelly, indicating descent from an original 'Ceallaigh', with the 'O' denoting 'grandson of.' The name was later anglicised to Kelly.

The prefix 'Mac' or 'Mc', meanwhile, as with the clans of the Scottish Highlands, denotes 'son of.'

Although the Irish clans had much in common with their Scottish counterparts, one important difference lies in what are known as 'septs', or branches, of the clan.

Septs of Scottish clans were groups who often bore an entirely different name from the clan name but were under the clan's protection.

In Ireland, septs were groups that shared the same name and who could be found scattered throughout the four provinces of Ulster, Leinster, Munster, and Connacht.

The 'golden age' of the Gaelic-Irish clans, infused as their veins were with the blood of Celts, pre-dates the Viking invasions of the eighth and ninth centuries and the Norman invasion of the twelfth century, and the sacred heart of the country was the Hill of Tara, near the River Boyne, in County Meath.

Known in Gaelic as 'Teamhar na Rí', or Hill of Kings, it was the royal seat of the 'Ard Rí Éireann', or High King of Ireland, to whom the petty kings, or chieftains, from the island's provinces were ultimately subordinate.

It was on the Hill of Tara, beside a stone pillar known as the Irish 'Lia Fáil', or Stone of Destiny, that the High Kings were inaugurated and, according to legend, this stone would emit a piercing screech that could be heard all over Ireland when touched by the hand of the rightful king.

The Hill of Tara is today one of the island's main tourist attractions.

Opposition to English rule over Ireland, established in the wake of the Cambro-Norman invasion, broke out frequently and the harsh solution adopted by the powerful forces of the Crown was to forcibly evict the native Irish from their lands.

These lands were then granted to Protestant colonists, or 'planters', from Britain.

Many of these colonists, ironically, came from Scotland and were the descendants of the original 'Scotti', or 'Scots', who gave their name to Scotland after migrating there in the fifth century A.D., from the north of Ireland.

Colonisation entailed harsh penal laws being imposed on the majority of the native Irish population, stripping them practically of all of their rights.

The Crown's main bastion in Ireland was Dublin and its environs, known as the Pale, and it was the dispossessed peasantry who lived outside this Pale, desperately striving to eke out a meagre living.

It was this that gave rise to the modern-day expression of someone or something being 'beyond the pale'.

Attempts were made to stamp out all aspects of the ancient Gaelic-Irish culture, to the extent that even to bear a Gaelic-Irish name was to invite discrimination.

This is why many Gaelic-Irish names were anglicised with, for example, and noted above, Ó Ceallaigh, or O'Kelly, being anglicised to Kelly.

Succeeding centuries have seen strong revivals of Gaelic-Irish consciousness, however, and this has led to many families reverting back to the original form of their name, while the language itself is frequently found on the fluent tongues of an estimated 90,000 to 145,000 of the island's population.

Ireland's turbulent history of religious and political strife is one that lasted well into the twentieth century, a landmark century that saw the partition of the island into the twenty-six counties of the independent Republic of

Ireland, or Eire, and the six counties of Northern Ireland, or Ulster.

Dublin, originally founded by Vikings, is now a vibrant and truly cosmopolitan city while the proud city of Belfast is one of the jewels in the crown of Ulster.

It was Saint Patrick who first brought the light of Christianity to Ireland in the fifth century A.D.

Interpretations of this Christian message have varied over the centuries, often leading to bitter sectarian conflict – but the many intricately sculpted Celtic Crosses found all over the island are symbolic of a unity that crosses the sectarian divide.

It is an image that fuses the 'old gods' of the Celts with Christianity.

All the signs from the early years of this new millennium indicate that sectarian strife may soon become a thing of the past – with the Irish and their many kinsfolk across the world, be they Protestant or Catholic, finding common purpose in the rich tapestry of their shared heritage.

Chapter two:

Warriors and bards

Unusual in that it has two distinctly different derivations, one Germanic and the other Gaelic Irish, the name of Ward has been present in Ireland from earliest times.

This was firstly in the original Gaelic form of Mac an Bháird, indicating 'son of the bard', or 'son of the poet', later anglicised to Ward, while following the late twelfth century Norman invasion of the island and the subsequent consolidation of the power of the English Crown, other 'Wards' settled on the island.

These original English and Scottish bearers of the Ward name derived it from the Saxon 'weard', meaning 'watchman', or 'guardian', while other sources assert it may derive from the Saxon 'werd', meaning 'marsh'.

Whatever the origin of their name, what is known for certain is that the English and Scottish Wards came to Ireland through the policy known as 'Plantation'.

Involving the settling of loyal subjects of the Crown on lands previously held by intransigent native Irish, it was started during the reign from 1491 to 1547 of Henry VIII, whose Reformation effectively outlawed the established Roman Catholic faith throughout his dominions.

This settlement of loyal Protestants in Ireland continued

throughout the subsequent reigns of Elizabeth I, James I (James VI of Scotland), and Charles I.

When these Wards arrived in Ireland, they found other bearers of the name, albeit as an anglicised version of Mac an Bháird, and whose bearers were heirs to an ancient and illustrious pedigree.

Ulster, one of the four provinces of the Emerald Isle, was the original homeland of the Mac an Bháirds, particularly modern day Co. Donegal, where there is the township of Lettermacward, although in about 300 A.D. some moved southwestwards to settle in Connacht, mainly in the area of Co. Galway.

With a history steeped in colourful and dramatic Celtic myth and legend, the Mac an Bháirds became one of the leading clans of the tribal grouping known as the Sodháin, based mainly at Muine Casáin, in what is now the parish of Baile mhic an Bháird, anglicised as Ballymacward.

As members of the Sodháin, they traced a proud descent from Connail Cearnach, better known as Conal of the Victories.

His father was Amairgen, famed for slaying a three-headed creature that dwelt in the underworld, while his mother was Findchaem, the daughter of a Druid known as Cathbad.

But it was as a first century A.D. chieftain of the Craobh Ruadh, or Red Branch Knights, that Connail Cearnach achieved his own fame.

Charged with the defence of the province of Ulster, the Red Branch Knights were an aristocratic military elite whose seat was at Emain Macha, an ancient hill fort whose ruins can be seen to this day about two miles west of Armagh.

Also the seat of the kings of Ulster, Emain Macha, or Fort Navan, boasted three great halls.

One was where the king and the Red Branch Knights feasted and slept, while another contained the province's treasury and a grisly display of the heads of slain enemies.

Finally there was the hall known as the speckled house, where the warriors' weapons were stored, while the *Bron-Bherg*, or Warrior's Sorrow, served as their hospital.

It was a descendant of Connail Cearnach, Sodhán Salbhuide, who took large numbers of his clan from Ulster to settle in Connacht, where they thrived for centuries as part of the powerful tribal grouping known as the Southern Uí Maine – honoured with the hereditary role of keepers of the horse for the Uí Maine kings.

But, although famed as warriors, it was as bards, in keeping with their original Gaelic name of Mac an Bháird, that they gained particular distinction and honour.

Bards played a vital role in Celtic society, responsible as they were for the composition and recital of the heroic deeds, glorious fortunes and tragic misfortunes of not only their own clans, but also other native Irish clans that they served in a hereditary role.

So great was the fame of the Wards as bards, that they

served in this role for a number of noted clans that included the O'Donnells, the MacMahons, the Maguires and the O'Neills.

In what became known as *Cogadh na Naoi mBliama*, or the Nine Years War, rebellion erupted in 1594 against the policy of plantation and the increasingly harsh treatment of the native Irish by the English Crown.

The rebels were defeated at the battle of Kinsale in 1601 and the rebellion finally suppressed three years later in Ulster.

Then, in September of 1607 and in what is known as The Flight of the Earls, Hugh O'Neill, 2nd Earl of Tyrone and Rory O'Donnell, 1st Earl of Tyrconnel, sailed into foreign exile from the village of Rathmullan, on the shore of Lough Swilly, in Co. Donegal, accompanied by ninety loyal followers.

Among them was Eoghan Ruadh Mac an Bháird, the bard to Rory O'Donnell, and who later wrote the haunting *A bhean fuair faill ar an bhfeart* – known in English as *Lament for the Earls of Tyrone and Tyrconnel*, and considered one of the finest poems of its kind in the Irish language.

In keeping with the famed literary and scholastic tradition of the Wards, Father Hugh Ward, known in his native Irish as Aedh Buidh Mac and Bháird, was the writer, historian and archaeologist who was born in 1590 in Lettermacward, Co. Donegal.

Not only recognised as the founder of Irish archaeology, he was also famously instrumental in arranging the exhaustive research for, and co-ordinating the writing of, the invaluable *The Annals of the Four Masters*, referred to on Page Six of this booklet.

A Franciscan priest and a professor of divinity at St Anthony's College, in Louvain, Belgium, it had been his original idea to gather together the material that came to form the *Annals*, while he was also instrumental in scouring the libraries of Europe in search of early Irish documents and records.

He died in 1635, less than a year before the *Annals* were completed.

Chapter three:

Battle honours

One of the inscriptions on the monument to the defenders of the Alamo, in San Antonio, Texas, reads: "William Ward of Ireland."

This refers to Lieutenant-Colonel William Ward, whose date of birth is unknown but who is known to have immigrated to the United States from his native Ireland as a young man.

Enlisting in the U.S. Army, he was later placed in command of the Georgia Battalion during the early nineteenth century Texas War of Independence with Mexico.

It was from between early February and early March of 1836 that the Alamo mission, near what is now modern day San Antonio, was attacked by up to 2,400 Mexican troops under the command of General López de Santa Anna.

Commanded by William Travis and Jim Bowie, the 260 defenders managed to repel the assault for thirteen days before finally being overwhelmed.

Only two defenders survived, with William Ward among the 256 dead.

Nearly 40 years later, in April of 1875, John Ward, born in 1848 in Arkansas and who died in 1911, became a recipient of the Medal of Honor – America's highest military award for bravery.

A Black Seminole Indian Scout, known as the Seminole Negro Indian Scouts, he was a sergeant during the Indian Wars of the Western United States when, in April of 1875, he led a successful charge against 25 of the enemy at the Pecos River, Texas.

One particularly adventurous bearer of the Ward name was the American sailor and soldier of fortune Frederick Townsend Ward, born in 1831 in Salem, Massachusetts.

Going to sea at an early age, by the time he was aged 20 he was First Mate aboard a ship trading to the coast of China.

Leaving the sea for a time, he settled in Mexico, but left after the failure of the scrap metal business he had set up.

Ever restless, he enlisted in the French Army to fight in the Crimean War of 1853 to 1856, but the headstrong Ward was dismissed from service for insubordination.

By 1860 he was in the bustling Chinese port of Shanghai, hired by the authorities to suppress river pirates, and later took command of the mercenary body at the service of Imperial China known as the Foreign Army Corps.

The corps, foreign mercenaries recruited from the Shanghai docks, was paid to protect Shanghai business interests during the Taiping Rebellion against Imperialist rule.

This corps, later augmented by Chinese conscripts trained by Ward, formed the nucleus of what later became renowned as The Ever Victorious Army.

Unfortunately for Ward, however, it was not always victorious, for he was killed in 1862 at the battle of Cixi, near Ningbo.

Three bearers of the ward name were recipients of the Victoria Cross (V.C.), the highest award for bravery in the face of enemy action for British and Commonwealth forces.

Born in 1823 in Harleston, Norfolk, Henry Ward had been a private in the 78th Regiment of Foot during the Indian Mutiny when, in September of 1857 at Lucknow, under heavy fire, he helped a wounded officer and a fellow private from the battlefield.

Later promoted to the rank of Quartermaster-General, he died in 1867.

Born in 1877 in Leeds, West Yorkshire, Charles Ward was a Boer War recipient of the V.C.

A private in the 2nd Battalion, The King's Own Yorkshire Light Infantry, it was in June of 1900 at Lindley, South Africa, that he volunteered to take an urgent message requesting reinforcements after a unit of his battalion was surrounded on three sides by a superior number of Boers.

Despite being severely wounded en route to his own lines, Ward managed to deliver the message, allowing reinforcements to come to the aid of his comrades.

Ward also has the distinction of having been the last recipient of the V.C. to be personally decorated with the honour by Queen Victoria.

Later achieving the rank of Company Sergeant-Major, he died in 1921, while rare film taken of him by the Lancashire cinema-photographers Sagar Mitchell and James Kenyon, shortly after he received his medal, was rediscovered by chance in 1994.

James Ward, born in 1919, was a New Zealand recipient of the V.C. for a particularly hair-raising act of bravery performed thousands of feet above the ground.

A sergeant in the Royal New Zealand Air Force serving with 75 (N.Z.) Squadron, Royal Air Force, during the Second World War, he had been the second pilot of a Vickers Wellington bomber returning from a raid on Munster, Germany, in July of 1941. Attacked by a German night-fighter, the bomber's starboard engine caught fire.

Ward, with the aid of a length of rope tied to the inner fuselage, gingerly crawled through a narrow hatch and onto the wing and managed to douse the flames.

He was killed in action over Hamburg 14 months later.

One posthumous recipient of America's Medal of Honor was another James Ward, born in 1921, in Springfield, Ohio.

A Seaman First Class, he had been aboard the U.S.S. Oklahoma when it came under Japanese attack at Pearl Harbor on December 7th, 1941.

Hit by three torpedo bombs, the battleship began to list dangerously, and the order was given to abandon ship before she capsized.

Ward remained in a gun turret to the last, holding a flashlight to allow the rest of the gun crew to make good their escape.

Also during the Second World War, Major General Orlando Ward was the highly decorated United States Army officer who commanded the U.S. 1st Armored Division during Operation Torch, the Allied landings in French North Africa in November of 1942.

Following the end of the war, Ward, who was born in 1891 and who graduated from West Point military academy in 1914, served for a time as Secretary to U.S. Army Chief of Staff George Marshall.

An expert in field artillery techniques and the recipient of honours that include the Distinguished Service Cross and the Silver Star, he died in 1972.

One distinguished British Army officer of the Second World War was General Sir Alfred Dudley Ward.

Born in 1905, his commands included that of the 5th Infantry Division in Italy, while he served for a time as Commander-in-Chief of the Northern Army Group and the British Army of the Rhine.

Appointed Governor and Commander-in-Chief of Gibraltar in 1962, his many awards include the Distinguished Service Order and the Legion of Merit, while Gibraltar's Dudley Ward Tunnel is named in his honour; he died in 1991.

From the destruction of the battlefield to the more

constructive world of business, James Kewley Ward, born in 1819 in Peel, Isle of Man, established a new life for himself in Canada, where he became a highly successful lumber merchant.

Immigrating firstly to the United States, at the age of 23, he trained in the lumber business in the New York State area before moving to Quebec in 1853 and operating a number of lumber enterprises.

Moving to Montreal in 1873, he opened the Mona Sawmills on the Lachine Canal.

He died in 1910, having previously donated $10,000 to build a public library in his birthplace of Peel; two postage stamps were issued in his honour by the Isle of Man in 1978.

From business to politics, John William Ward, 1st Earl of Dudley, born in 1781 and who died in 1833, served as Britain's Foreign Secretary from 1823 to 1827.

In New Zealand, Sir Joseph Ward, born of Irish stock in 1856, rose from helping to run his mother's boarding house and working as a postal clerk to serve as Prime Minister of New Zealand from 1906 to 1912 and from 1928 until his death in 1930.

Chapter four:
On the world stage

From acting and sport to music and art, bearers of the Ward name have gained distinction and fame at an international level.

Born in 1941 in Beckenham, Kent, **Simon Ward** is the English stage and film actor who, after training at London's Royal Academy of Dramatic Arts, first rose to prominence at the age of 26 for his role in the Joe Orton play *Loot*.

International acclaim followed for his roles in a succession of films, most notably the 1972 *Young Winston*, the 1973 *The Three Musketeers*, the 1979 *Zulu Dawn* and, from 1989, *Around the World in 80 Days*.

Still active on the stage, he also took the title role in Alan Bennett's play *The Madness of King George III*.

Keeping acting in the family, his daughter, **Sophie Ward**, born in London in 1964, is the stage and screen actress whose film credits include the 1985 *Little Dorit* and the 2008 *Book of Blood*, while she has also appeared in British television productions that include *Heartbeat* and the medical drama *Holby City*.

With roles that include the 2001 *Pink Pyjamas* and the 2011 *Pirates of the Caribbean: On Stranger Tides*, **Gemma Ward** is the model and actress who was born in 1987 in Perth, Western Australia.

Best known for his role as Robin in the cult *Batman* television series from 1966 to 1968, **Burt Ward** is the American actor who was actually born Bert John Gervis, Jr.

Dropping 'Bert' in favour of Burt, the actor, born in Los Angeles in 1945, also adopted his mother's maiden name of Ward.

Best known for his role from 2003 to 2007 as the builder Charlie Stubbs in the popular British television soap *Coronation Street*, **Bill Ward** is the English actor born in 1967 in Newcastle upon Tyne.

'Killed off' in the soap when he was murdered by his lover, the scene won Best Exit and Best Storyline at the 2007 British Soap Awards.

Behind the camera lens, **David Ward**, born in 1945 in Providence, Rhode Island, is the American film director and screenwriter whose screenplay for the 1974 *The Sting* won an Oscar for Best Original Screenplay.

Other screenplay credits include, along with Nola Ephron, *Sleepless in Seattle* and, from 2006, *Flyboys*.

Screenwriter of a number of documentaries on aspects of American history, **Geoffrey Ward**, born in 1940, is the American historian who wrote the television mini-series *The Civil War*, in addition to winning a National Book Critics Circle Award for his biography of American President Franklin Delano Roosevelt.

From film to the highly competitive world of sport, **Charlie Ward**, born in Birmingham in 1911 and who died in 2001, was the leading British golfer of the 1940s who won the British Order of Merit in both 1948 and 1949 and represented his country in the Ryder Cup on no less than three occasions.

In the Canadian national sport of ice hockey, **Aaron Ward**, born in 1973 in Windsor, Ontario is the former defenceman of the National Hockey League (NHL) who was thrice a member of teams that won the prestigious Stanley Cup.

This was with the Detroit Red Wings in 1997 and 1998 and with the Carolina Hurricanes in 2006.

Also on the ice, Cameron Ward, better known as **Cam Ward**, born in 1984 in Saskatoon, Saskatchewan, was the goaltender for the Carolina Hurricanes team that won the 2006 Stanley Cup.

Bearers of the Ward name have also excelled in the bruising world of boxing – no less so than the former junior welterweight boxer **Micky Ward**.

Born of Irish stock in 1965 in Lowell, Massachusetts and nicknamed "Irish", he is best known in the annals of boxing for three memorable contests he had with the late Arturo Gatti.

His first encounter with Gatti, known as Ward-Gatti I, and which Ward won, took place in May of 2002 and was hailed as "the fight of the century."

The boxers met again in November of that year in Ward-Gatti II, a contest that Ward lost as he also narrowly did in Ward-Gatti III in June of 2003 – an encounter named as "fight of the year."

A biography of Ward, *Irish Thunder: The Hard Life and Times of Micky Ward* was written by Bob Halloran, while a film, *The Fighter*, was released in 2010 with Mark Wahlberg in the role of Ward.

In contemporary boxing, **Andre Ward**, born in 1984 in San Francisco and nicknamed "Son of God", is the American boxer who won a gold medal at the 2004 Olympics in the light heavyweight division and who, at the time of writing, is the World Boxing Association's super middleweight champion.

From boxing to tennis, **Holcombe Ward**, born in New York in 1878, was the American player who won the men's single title at the 1904 U.S. Championship and who, between 1899 and 1906, was a U.S. Doubles champion. An inductee of the International Tennis Hall of Fame, he died in 1967.

On the cricket pitch, **Alan Ward**, born in 1947 in Dronfield, Derbyshire is the former English right-arm bowler who played for both Derbyshire and Leicestershire and in five Test Matches from 1969 to 1976.

In the high speed sport of race-car driving, **Rodger Ward**, born in 1921 in Beloit, Kansas, and who died in 2004, was the Second World War fighter pilot who won both the 1959 and the 1962 Indianapolis 500.

From sport to the world of music, **Bill Ward** is the English drummer, born in 1948 in Aston, Birmingham, who, along with Geezer Butler, Tony Iommi and Ozzy Osbourne, was a founding member of the heavy metal rock band Black Sabbath.

Yet another noted drummer is **Andy Ward**, born in 1952 in Epsom, Surrey and a founding member of the British progressive rock band Camel – memorably known for a performance they gave in London's Royal Albert Hall in 1975 of their album *The Snow Goose* - accompanied by the London Symphony Orchestra.

A teacher of English and drama before embarking on a highly successful career as a singer and songwriter, Clifford Thomas Ward, better known as **Clifford T. Ward**, was born in 1944 in Stourport-on-Severn, Worcestershire.

Best remembered for his 1973 international hit *Gaye*, he also penned songs for a range of artistes who include Cliff Richard, Jack Jones, Art Garfunkel and Judy Collins; he died in 2001.

Best known as the bass guitarist from 1989 to 1996 of the American punk rock band The Ramones, Christopher Joseph Ward, born in 1965 in Queens, New York City, is the American musician better known as **C.J. Ramone**, while Alasdair Ward, better known as **Algy Ward**, is an English bass guitarist and singer.

Born in 1959 in Croydon, Surrey, he played for a time with the British punk band The Damned, before founding the heavy metal band Tank in the early 1980s.

In contemporary pop music, **Shayne Ward**, born of

Irish parentage in Clayton, Manchester, in 1984, is the English singer who first rose to fame after winning the 2005 series of the talent show *The X-Factor*, and who has since enjoyed a number of single and album hits.

In the creative world of art, **Bernard Evans Ward**, born in 1857, was the distinguished painter of the Victorian era whose works, such as *Huldra's Nymphs*, were regularly exhibited at the Royal Society of British Artists, in his native London.

Immigrating to the United States in 1913 after a lawsuit resulted in the loss of his financial fortune, he settled in Cleveland, Ohio, where his daughter worked as a correspondent for a London newspaper.

Ward soon made a name for himself in his adopted country as a portrait artist, living for a time in Florida before returning to Ohio, where he died in 1933.

Inducted in 1989 into America's Academy of Adventure Gaming Arts and Design Hall of Fame, James M. Ward, better known as **Jim Ward**, is the game designer and fantasy author who was born in 1951.

Author of a number of books that include his 2007 *Time Twisters Anthology*, he also gave his name to the *Dungeons and Dragons* character 'Drawmij' – his name spelled backwards.

One particularly unfortunate bearer of the Ward name was the nineteenth century Irish scientist **Mary Ward**.

Born in 1827 in Ballylin, Co. Offaly, into a family of

eminent scholars and scientists, the prejudices of the time meant that a university education was denied to women.

Undaunted, as a teenager she immersed herself in scientific study by corresponding with scientific bodies and carrying out her own meticulous research – particularly in the fields of studying insect life under the microscope and astronomy.

At the age of 31, she published what was to be the first of several books, *Sketches with the Microscope*.

Her cousin, William Parsons, 3rd Earl of Rosse, who carried out his own astronomical studies from an observatory on his Co. Offaly estate, had two sons who were also interested in scientific study and technical invention.

The sons had built a steam-powered automobile, and it was in this that an excited Mary Ward and her husband, the 5th Viscount Bangor, were travelling in August of 1869, through the Parsons estate.

Thrown from the vehicle as it rounded a bend and falling under one of its steel wheels, she was killed instantly – giving her the unenviable distinction of being the first recorded victim of a motor vehicle accident.

Key dates in Ireland's history from the first settlers to the formation of the Irish Republic:

circa 7000 B.C. Arrival and settlement of Stone Age people.

circa 3000 B.C. Arrival of settlers of New Stone Age period.

circa 600 B.C. First arrival of the Celts.

200 A.D. Establishment of Hill of Tara, Co. Meath, as seat of the High Kings.

circa 432 A.D. Christian mission of St. Patrick.

800-920 A.D. Invasion and subsequent settlement of Vikings.

1002 A.D. Brian Boru recognised as High King.

1014 Brian Boru killed at battle of Clontarf.

1169-1170 Cambro-Norman invasion of the island.

1171 Henry II claims Ireland for the English Crown.

1366 Statutes of Kilkenny ban marriage between native Irish and English.

1529-1536 England's Henry VIII embarks on religious Reformation.

1536 Earl of Kildare rebels against the Crown.

1541 Henry VIII declared King of Ireland.

1558 Accession to English throne of Elizabeth I.

1565 Battle of Affane.

1569-1573 First Desmond Rebellion.

1579-1583 Second Desmond Rebellion.

1594-1603 Nine Years War.

1606 Plantation' of Scottish and English settlers.

1607	Flight of the Earls.
1632-1636	Annals of the Four Masters compiled.
1641	Rebellion over policy of plantation and other grievances.
1649	Beginning of Cromwellian conquest.
1688	Flight into exile in France of Catholic Stuart monarch James II as Protestant Prince William of Orange invited to take throne of England along with his wife, Mary.
1689	William and Mary enthroned as joint monarchs; siege of Derry.
1690	Jacobite forces of James defeated by William at battle of the Boyne (July) and Dublin taken.
1691	Athlone taken by William; Jacobite defeats follow at Aughrim, Galway, and Limerick; conflict ends with Treaty of Limerick (October) and Irish officers allowed to leave for France.
1695	Penal laws introduced to restrict rights of Catholics; banishment of Catholic clergy.
1704	Laws introduced constricting rights of Catholics in landholding and public office.
1728	Franchise removed from Catholics.
1791	Foundation of United Irishmen republican movement.
1796	French invasion force lands in Bantry Bay.
1798	Defeat of Rising in Wexford and death of United Irishmen leaders Wolfe Tone and Lord Edward Fitzgerald.

1800	Act of Union between England and Ireland.
1803	Dublin Rising under Robert Emmet.
1829	Catholics allowed to sit in Parliament.
1845-1849	The Great Hunger: thousands starve to death as potato crop fails and thousands more emigrate.
1856	Phoenix Society founded.
1858	Irish Republican Brotherhood established.
1873	Foundation of Home Rule League.
1893	Foundation of Gaelic League.
1904	Foundation of Irish Reform Association.
1913	Dublin strikes and lockout.
1916	Easter Rising in Dublin and proclamation of an Irish Republic.
1917	Irish Parliament formed after Sinn Fein election victory.
1919-1921	War between Irish Republican Army and British Army.
1922	Irish Free State founded, while six northern counties remain part of United Kingdom as Northern Ireland, or Ulster; civil war up until 1923 between rival republican groups.
1949	Foundation of Irish Republic after all remaining constitutional links with Britain are severed.